W9-CMZ-435
WITHDRAWN

CHRISTINA ROSSETTI

Selected Poems

BLOOMSBURY
* POETRY *
CLASSICS

St. Martin's Press
New York

BLOOMSBURY POETRY CLASSICS: CHRISTINA ROSSETTI: SELECTED POEMS.

For information, address St. Martin's Press,
175 Fifth Avenue, New York, N.Y. 10010.

Selection by Ian Hamilton
Jacket design by Jeff Fisher

ISBN 0-312-13437-1

First published in Great Britain by Bloomsbury Publishing Ltd.

First U.S. Edition: September 1995
10 9 8 7 6 5 4 3 2 1

CONTENTS

GONE FOR EVER

O happy rose-bud blooming
  Upon thy parent tree,
Nay, thou art too presuming;
For soon the earth entombing
  Thy faded charms shall be,
And the chill damp consuming.

O happy skylark springing
  Up to the broad blue sky,
Too fearless in thy winging,
Too gladsome in thy singing,
  Thou also soon shalt lie
Where no sweet notes are ringing.

And through life's shine and shower
  We shall have joy and pain;
But in the summer bower,
And at the morning hour,
  We still shall look in vain
For the same bird and flower.

VANITY OF VANITIES

Ah woe is me for pleasure that is vain,
  Ah woe is me for glory that is past:
  Pleasure that bringeth sorrow at the last,
Glory that at the last bringeth no gain!
So saith the sinking heart; and so again
  It shall say till the mighty angel-blast
  Is blown, making the sun and moon aghast,
And showering down the stars like sudden rain.
And evermore men shall go fearfully
  Bending beneath their weight of heaviness;
And ancient men shall lie down wearily,
  And strong men shall rise up in weariness;
Yea, even the young shall answer sighingly,
  Saying one to another: How vain it is!

A PAUSE OF THOUGHT

I looked for that which is not, nor can be,
  And hope deferred made my heart sick in truth:
  But years must pass before a hope of youth
    Is resigned utterly.

I watched and waited with a steadfast will:
  And though the object seemed to flee away

That I so longed for, ever day by day
  I watched and waited still.

Sometimes I said: This thing shall be no more;
  My expectation wearies and shall cease;
  I will resign it now and be at peace:
    Yet never gave it o'er.

Sometimes I said: It is an empty name
  I long for; to a name why should I give
  The peace of all the days I have to live? –
    Yet gave it all the same.

Alas, thou foolish one! alike unfit
  For healthy joy and salutary pain:
  Thou knowest the chase useless, and again
    Turnest to follow it.

SONG

When I am dead, my dearest,
  Sing no sad songs for me;
Plant thou no roses at my head,
  Nor shady cypress tree:
Be the green grass above me
  With showers and dewdrops wet;
And if thou wilt, remember,
  And if thou wilt, forget.

I shall not see the shadows,
  I shall not feel the rain;
I shall not hear the nightingale
  Sing on, as if in pain:
And dreaming through the twilight
  That doth not rise nor set,
Haply I may remember,
  And haply may forget.

AFTER DEATH

The curtains were half drawn, the floor was swept
  And strewn with rushes, rosemary and may
  Lay thick upon the bed on which I lay,
Where thro' the lattice ivy-shadows crept.
He leaned above me, thinking that I slept
  And could not hear him; but I heard him say:
  "Poor child, poor child:" and as he turned away
Came a deep silence, and I knew he wept.
He did not touch the shroud, or raise the fold
  That hid my face, or take my hand in his,
    Or ruffle the smooth pillows for my head:
    He did not love me living; but once dead
  He pitied me; and very sweet it is
To know he still is warm tho' I am cold.

REMEMBER

Remember me when I am gone away,
  Gone far away into the silent land;
  When you can no more hold me by the hand,
Nor I half turn to go yet turning stay.
Remember me when no more day by day
  You tell me of our future that you planned:
  Only remember me; you understand
It will be late to counsel then or pray.
Yet if you should forget me for a while
  And afterwards remember, do not grieve:
  For if the darkness and corruption leave
  A vestige of the thoughts that once I had,
Better by far you should forget and smile
  Than that you should remember and be sad.

REST

O Earth, lie heavily upon her eyes;
  Seal her sweet eyes weary of watching, Earth;
  Lie close around her; leave no room for mirth
With its harsh laughter, nor for sound of sighs.
She hath no questions, she hath no replies,
  Hushed in and curtained with a blessèd dearth
  Of all that irked her from the hour of birth;
With stillness that is almost Paradise.
Darkness more clear than noon-day holdeth her,
  Silence more musical than any song;
Even her very heart has ceased to stir:
Until the morning of Eternity
Her rest shall not begin nor end, but be;
  And when she wakes she will not think it long.

SONG

Oh roses for the flush of youth,
  And laurel for the perfect prime;
But pluck an ivy branch for me
    Grown old before my time.

Oh violets for the grave of youth,
  And bay for those dead in their prime;
Give me the withered leaves I chose
    Before in the old time.

ONE CERTAINTY

Vanity of vanities, the Preacher saith,
  All things are vanity. The eye and ear
  Cannot be filled with what they see and hear.
Like early dew, or like the sudden breath
Of wind, or like the grass that withereth,
  Is man, tossed to and fro by hope and fear:
  So little joy hath he, so little cheer,
Till all things end in the long dust of death.
Today is still the same as yesterday,
  Tomorrow also even as one of them;
And there is nothing new under the sun:
Until the ancient race of Time be run,
  The old thorns shall grow out of the old stem,
And morning shall be cold and twilight grey.

SWEET DEATH

The sweetest blossoms die.
  And so it was that, going day by day
  Unto the Church to praise and pray,
And crossing the green churchyard thoughtfully,
  I saw how on the graves the flowers
  Shed their fresh leaves in showers,
And how their perfume rose up to the sky
  Before it passed away.

The youngest blossoms die.
  They die and fall and nourish the rich earth
  From which they lately had their birth;
Sweet life, but sweeter death that passeth by
  And is as though it had not been: —
  All colours turn to green;
The bright hues vanish and the odours fly,
  The grass hath lasting worth.

And youth and beauty die.
  So be it, O my God, Thou God of truth:
  Better than beauty and than youth
Are Saints and Angels, a glad company;
  And Thou, O Lord, our Rest and Ease,
  Art better far than these.
Why should we shrink from our full harvest? why
  Prefer to glean with Ruth?

A TESTIMONY

I said of laughter: it is vain.
  Of mirth I said: what profits it?
  Therefore I found a book, and writ
Therein how ease and also pain,
How health and sickness, every one
Is vanity beneath the sun

Man walks in a vain shadow; he
  Disquieteth himself in vain.
  The things that were shall be again:
The rivers do not fill the sea,
But turn back to their secret source;
The winds too turn upon their course.

Our treasures moth and rust corrupt,
  Or thieves break thro' and steal, or they
  Make themselves wings and fly away.
One man made merry as he supped,
Nor guessed how when that night grew dim
His soul would be required of him.

We build our houses on the sand
  Comely withoutside and within;
  But when the winds and rains begin
  To beat on them, they cannot stand:

They perish, quickly overthrown,
Loose from the very basement stone.

All things are vanity, I said:
  Yea vanity of vanities.
  The rich man dies; and the poor dies:
The worm feeds sweetly on the dead.
Whate'er thou lackest, keep this trust:
All in the end shall have but dust:

The one inheritance, which best
  And worst alike shall find and share:
  The wicked cease from troubling there,
And there the weary be at rest;
There all the wisdom of the wise
Is vanity of vanities.

Man flourishes as a green leaf,
  And as a leaf doth pass away;
  Or as a shade that cannot stay
And leaves no track, his course is brief:
Yet man doth hope and fear and plan
Till he is dead: — oh foolish man!

Our eyes cannot be satisfied
  With seeing, nor our ears be filled
  With hearing: yet we plant and build
And buy and make our borders wide;

We gather wealth, we gather care,
But know not who shall be our heir.

Why should we hasten to arise
  So early, and so late take rest?
  Our labour is not good; our best
Hopes fade; our heart is stayed on lies:
Verily, we sow wind; and we
Shall reap the whirlwind, verily.

He who hath little shall not lack;
  He who hath plenty shall decay:
  Our fathers went; we pass away;
Our children follow on our track:
So generations fail, and so
They are renewed and come and go.

The earth is fattened with our dead;
  She swallows more and doth not cease:
  Therefore her wine and oil increase
And her sheaves are not numberèd;
Therefore her plants are green, and all
Her pleasant trees lusty and tall.

Therefore the maidens cease to sing,
  And the young men are very sad;
  Therefore the sowing is not glad,

And mournful is the harvesting.
Of high and low, of great and small,
Vanity is the lot of all.

A King dwelt in Jerusalem;
  He was the wisest man on earth;
  He had all the riches from his birth,
And pleasures till he tired of them;
Then, having tested all things, he
Witnessed that all are vanity.

SYMBOLS

I watched a rosebud very long
   Brought on by dew and sun and shower,
   Waiting to see the perfect flower:
Then, when I thought it should be strong,
   It opened at the matin hour
      And fell at evensong.

I watched a nest from day to day,
   A green nest full of pleasant shade,
   Wherein three speckled eggs were laid:
But when they should have hatched in May,
   The two old birds had grown afraid
      Or tired, and flew away.

Then in my wrath I broke the bough
   That I had tended so with care,
   Hoping its scent should fill the air;
I crushed the eggs, not heeding how
   Their ancient promise had been fair:
      I would have vengeance now.

But the dead branch spoke from the sod,
   And the eggs answered me again:
   Because we failed dost thou complain?
Is thy wrath just? And what if God,

Who waiteth for thy fruits in vain,
  Should also take the rod?

TWILIGHT CALM

Oh pleasant eventide!
Clouds on the western side
Grow grey and greyer hiding the warm sun:
The bees and birds, their happy labours done,
Seek their close nests and bide.

Screened in the leafy wood
The stock-doves sit and brood:
The very squirrel leaps from bough to bough
But lazily; pauses; and settles now
Where once he stored his food.

One by one the flowers close,
Lily and dewy rose
Shutting their tender petals from the moon:
The grasshoppers are still, but not so soon
Are still the noisy crows.

The dormouse squats and eats
Choice little dainty bits
Beneath the spreading roots of a broad lime;
Nibbling his fill he stops from time to time
And listens where he sits.

From far the lowings come
Of cattle driven home:
From farther still the wind brings fitfully
The vast continual murmur of the sea,
Now loud, now almost dumb.

The gnats whirl in the air,
The evening gnats; and there
The owl opes broad his eyes and wings to sail
For prey; the bat wakes; and the shell-less snail
Comes forth, clammy and bare.

Hark! that's the nightingale,
Telling the selfsame tale
Her song told when this ancient earth was young:
So echoes answered when her song was sung
In the first wooded vale.

We call it love and pain
The passion of her strain;
And yet we little understand or know:
Why should it not be rather joy that so
Throbs in each throbbing vein?

In separate herds the deer
Lie; here the bucks, and here
The does, and by its mother sleeps the fawn:
Through all the hours of night until the dawn
They sleep, forgetting fear.

The hare sleeps where it lies,
With wary half-closed eyes;
The cock has ceased to crow, the hen to cluck:
Only the fox is out, some heedless duck
Or chicken to surprise.

Remote, each single star
Comes out, till there they are
All shining brightly: how the dews fall damp!
While close at hand the glow-worm lights her lamp
Or twinkles from afar.

But evening now is done
As much as if the sun
Day-giving had arisen in the East:
For night has come; and the great calm has ceased,
The quiet sands have run.

A FAIR WORLD THOUGH A FALLEN

You tell me that the world is fair, in spite
    Of the old Fall; and that I should not turn
  So to the grave, and let my spirit yearn
After the quiet of the long last night.
Have I then shut mine eyes against the light,
  Grief-deafened lest my spirit should discern?
  Yet how could I keep silence when I burn?
And who can give me comfort?—Hear the right.
Have patience with the weak and sick at heart:
  Bind up the wounded with a tender touch,
    Comfort the sad, tear-blinded as they go:—
For, though I failed to choose the better part,
    Were it a less unutterable woe
  If we should come to love this world too much?

ECHO

Come to me in the silence of the night;
  Come in the speaking silence of a dream;
Come with soft rounded cheeks and eyes as bright
  As sunlight on a stream;
    Come back in tears,
O memory, hope, love of finished years.

Oh dream how sweet, too sweet, too bitter sweet,
  Whose wakening should have been in Paradise,
Where souls brimfull of love abide and meet;
  Where thirsting longing eyes
    Watch the slow door
That opening, letting in, lets out no more.

Yet come to me in dreams, that I may live
  My very life again tho' cold in death:
Come back to me in dreams, that I may give
  Pulse for pulse, breath for breath:
    Speak low, lean low,
As long ago, my love, how long ago.

THE BOURNE

Underneath the growing grass,
  Underneath the living flowers,
  Deeper than the sound of showers:
  There we shall not count the hours
By the shadows as they pass.

Youth and health will be but vain,
  Beauty reckoned of no worth:
  There a very little girth
  Can hold round what once the earth
Seemed too narrow to contain.

FROM THE ANTIQUE

It's a weary life, it is, she said: —
  Doubly blank in a woman's lot:
I wish and I wish I were a man:
  Or, better than any being, were not:

Were nothing at all in all the world,
  Not a body and not a soul:
Not so much as a grain of dust
  Or a drop of water from pole to pole.

Still the world would wag on the same,
  Still the seasons go and come:
Blossoms bloom as in days of old,
  Cherries ripen and wild bees hum.

None would miss me in all the world,
  How much less would care or weep:
I should be nothing, while all the rest
  Would wake and weary and fall asleep.

MAY

I cannot tell you how it was;
But this I know: it came to pass
Upon a bright and breezy day
When May was young; ah pleasant May!
As yet the poppies were not born
Between the blades of tender corn;
The last eggs had not hatched as yet,
Nor any bird foregone its mate.

I cannot tell you what it was;
But this I know: it did but pass.
It passed away with sunny May,
With all sweet things it passed away,
And left me old, and cold, and grey.

A TRIAD

Three sang of love together: one with lips
  Crimson, with cheeks and bosom in a glow,
Flushed to the yellow hair and finger tips;
  And one there sang who soft and smooth as
      snow
  Bloomed like a tinted hyacinth at a show;
And one was blue with famine after love,
  Who like a harpstring snapped rang harsh and
      low
The burden of what those were singing of.
One shamed herself in love; one temperately
  Grew gross in soulless love, a sluggish wife;
One famished died for love. Thus two of three
  Took death for love and won him afterstrife;
One droned in sweetness like a fattened bee:
  All on the threshold, yet all short of life.

SHUT OUT

The door was shut. I looked between
   Its iron bars; and saw it lie,
   My garden, mine, beneath the sky,
Pied with all flowers bedewed and green:

From bough to bough the song-birds crossed,
   From flower to flower the moths and bees;
   With all its nests and stately trees
It had been mine, and it was lost.

A shadowless spirit kept the gate,
   Blank and unchanging like the grave.
   I peering thro' said: "Let me have
Some buds to cheer my outcast state."

He answered not. "Or give me, then,
   But one small twig from shrub or tree;
   And bid my home remember me
Until I come to it again."

The spirit was silent; but he took
   Mortar and stone to build a wall;
   He left no loophole great or small
Thro' which my straining eyes might look:

So now I sit here quite alone
  Blinded with tears; nor grieve for that,
  For nought is left worth looking at
Since my delightful land is gone.

A violet bed is budding near,
  Wherein a lark has made her nest:
  And good they are, but not the best;
And dear they are, but not so dear.

A BETTER RESURRECTION

I have no wit, no words, no tears;
  My heart within me like a stone
Is numbed too much for hopes or fears;
  Look right, look left, I dwell alone;
I lift mine eyes, but dimmed with grief
  No everlasting hills I see;
My life is in the falling leaf:
    O Jesus, quicken me.

My life is like a faded leaf,
  My harvest dwindled to a husk;
Truly my life is void and brief
  And tedious in the barren dusk;
My life is like a frozen thing,
  No bud nor greenness can I see:
Yet rise it shall — the sap of Spring;
    O Jesus, rise in me.

My life is like a broken bowl,
  A broken bowl that cannot hold
One drop of water for my soul
  Or cordial in the searching cold;
Cast in the fire the perished thing,
  Melt and remould it, till it be
A royal cup for Him my King:
    O Jesus, drink of me.

WINTER: MY SECRET

I tell my secret? No indeed, not I:
Perhaps some day, who knows?
But not today; it froze, and blows, and snows,
And you're too curious: fie!
You want to hear it? well:
Only, my secret's mine, and I won't tell.

Or, after all, perhaps there's none:
Suppose there is no secret after all,
But only just my fun.
Today's a nipping day, a biting day;
In which one wants a shawl,
A veil, a cloak, and other wraps:
I cannot ope to every one who taps,
And let the draughts come whistling thro' my hall;
Come bounding and surrounding me,
Come buffeting, astounding me,
Nipping and clipping thro' my wraps and all.
I wear my mask for warmth: who ever shows
His nose to Russian snows
To be pecked at by every wind that blows?
You would not peck? I thank you for good will,
Believe, but leave that truth untested still.

Spring's an expansive time: yet I don't trust
March with its peck of dust,
Nor April with its rainbow-crowned brief showers,
Nor even May, whose flowers
One frost may wither thro' the sunless hours.

Perhaps some languid summer day,
When drowsy birds sing less and less,
And golden fruit is ripening to excess,
If there's not too much sun nor too much cloud,
And the warm wind is neither still nor loud,
Perhaps my secret I may say,
Or you may guess.

AN APPLE-GATHERING

I plucked pink blossoms from mine apple tree
  And wore them all that evening in my hair:
Then in due season when I went to see
    I found no apples there.

With dangling basket all along the grass
  As I had come I went the selfsame track:
My neighbours mocked me while they saw me pass
    So empty-handed back.

Lilian and Lilias smiled in trudging by,
  Their heaped-up basket teazed me like a jeer;
Sweet-voiced they sang beneath the sunset sky,
    Their mother's home was near.

Plump Gertrude passed me with her basket full,
  A stronger hand than hers helped it along;
A voice talked with her thro' the shadows cool
    More sweet to me than song.

Ah Willie, Willie, was my love less worth
  Than apples with their green leaves piled above?
I counted rosiest apples on the earth
    Of far less worth than love.

So once it was with me you stooped to talk
   Laughing and listening in this very lane:
To think that by this way we used to walk
      We shall not walk again!

I let my neighbours pass me, ones and twos
   And groups; the latest said the night grew chill,
And hastened: but I loitered, while the dews
      Fell fast I loitered still.

MEMORY

I

I nursed it in my bosom while it lived,
  I hid it in my heart when it was dead;
In joy I sat alone, even so I grieved
    Alone and nothing said.

I shut the door to face the naked truth,
  I stood alone—I faced the truth alone,
Stripped bare of self-regard or forms or ruth
    Till first and last were shown.

I took the perfect balances and weighed;
  No shaking of my hand disturbed the poise;
Weighed, found it wanting: not a word I said,
    But silent made my choice.

None know the choice I made; I make it still.
  None know the choice I made and broke my
      heart,
Breaking mine idol: I have braced my will
    Once, chosen for once my part.

I broke it at a blow, I laid it cold,
  Crushed in my deep heart where it used to live.
My heart dies inch by inch; the time grows old,
    Grows old in which I grieve.

II

I have a room whereinto no one enters
    Save I myself alone:
    There sits a blessed memory on a throne,
There my life centres;

While winter comes and goes — oh tedious comer! —
    And while its nip-wind blows;
    While bloom the bloodless lily and warm rose
Of lavish summer.

If any should force entrance he might see there
    One buried yet not dead,
    Before whose face I no more bow my head
Or bend my knee there;

But often in my worn life's autumn weather
    I watch there with clear eyes,
    And think how it will be in Paradise
When we're together.

A BIRTHDAY

My heart is like a singing bird
  Whose nest is in a watered shoot;
My heart is like an apple tree
  Whose boughs are bent with thickset fruit;
My heart is like a rainbow shell
  That paddles in a halcyon sea;
My heart is gladder than all these
  Because my love is come to me.

Raise me a dais of silk and down;
  Hang it with vair and purple dyes;
Carve it in doves and pomegranates,
  And peacocks with a hundred eyes;
Work it in gold and silver grapes,
  In leaves and silver fleurs-de-lys;
Because the birthday of my life
  Is come, my love is come to me.

"THE LOVE OF CHRIST WHICH PASSETH KNOWLEDGE"

I bore with thee long weary days and nights,
   Through many pangs of heart, through many
      tears;
I bore with thee, thy hardness, coldness, slights,
      For three and thirty years.

Who else had dared for thee what I have dared?
   I plunged the depth most deep from bliss above;
I not My flesh, I not My Spirit spared:
      Give thou Me love for love.

For thee I thirsted in the daily drouth,
   For thee I trembled in the nightly frost:
Much sweeter thou than honey to My mouth:
      Why wilt thou still be lost?

I bore thee on My shoulders and rejoiced:
   Men only marked upon My shoulders borne
The branding cross; and shouted hungry-voiced,
      Or wagged their heads in scorn.

Thee did nails grave upon My hands, thy name
   Did thorns for frontlets stamp between Mine
      eyes:

I, Holy One, put on thy guilt and shame;
    I, God, Priest, Sacrifice.

A thief upon My right hand and My left;
  Six hours alone, athirst, in misery:
At length in death one smote My heart and cleft
    A hiding-place for thee.

Nailed to the racking cross, than bed of down
  More dear, whereon to stretch Myself and sleep:
So did I win a kingdom, — share My crown;
    A harvest, — come and reap.

BY THE SEA

Why does the sea moan evermore?
  Shut out from heaven it makes its moan,
It frets against the boundary shore;
  All earth's full rivers cannot fill
  The sea, that drinking thirsteth still.

Sheer miracles of loveliness
  Lie hid in its unlooked-on bed:
Anemones, salt, passionless,
  Blow flower-like; just enough alive
  To blow and multiply and thrive.

Shells quaint with curve, or spot, or spike,
  Encrusted live things argus-eyed,
All fair alike, yet all unlike,
  Are born without a pang, and die
  Without a pang, and so pass by.

UP-HILL

Does the road wind up-hill all the way?
  Yes, to the very end.
Will the day's journey take the whole long day?
  From morn to night, my friend.

But is there for the night a resting-place?
  A roof for when the slow dark hours begin.
May not the darkness hide it from my face?
  You cannot miss that inn.

Shall I meet other wayfarers at night?
  Those who have gone before.
Then must I knock, or call when just in sight?
  They will not keep you standing at that door.

Shall I find comfort, travel-sore and weak?
  Of labour you shall find the sum.
Will there be beds for me and all who seek?
  Yea, beds for all who come.

THE CONVENT THRESHOLD

There's blood between us, love, my love,
There's father's blood, there's brother's blood;
And blood's a bar I cannot pass:
I choose the stairs that mount above,
Stair after golden skyward stair,
To city and to sea of glass.
My lily feet are soiled with mud,
With scarlet mud which tells a tale
Of hope that was, of guilt that was,
Of love that shall not yet avail;
Alas, my heart, if I could bare
My heart, this selfsame stain is there:
I seek the sea of glass and fire
To wash the spot, to burn the snare;
Lo, stairs are meant to lift us higher:
Mount with me, mount the kindled stair.

Your eyes look earthward, mine look up.
I see the far-off city grand,
Beyond the hills a watered land,
Beyond the gulf a gleaming strand
Of mansions where the righteous sup;
Who sleep at ease among their trees,
Or wake to sing a cadenced hymn
With Cherubim and Seraphim;

They bore the Cross, they drained the cup,
Racked, roasted, crushed, wrenched limb from limb,
They the offscouring of the world:
The heaven of starry heavens unfurled,
The sun before their face is dim.

You looking earthward, what see you?
Milk-white, wine-flushed among the vines,
Up and down leaping, to and fro,
Most glad, most full, made strong with wines,
Blooming as peaches pearled with dew,
Their golden windy hair afloat,
Love-music warbling in their throat,
Young men and women come and go.

You linger, yet the time is short:
Flee for your life, gird up your strength
To flee; the shadows stretched at length
Show that day wanes, that night draws nigh;
Flee to the mountain, tarry not.

Is this a time for smile and sigh,
For songs among the secret trees
Where sudden blue birds nest and sport?
The time is short and yet you stay:
Today while it is called today
Kneel, wrestle, knock, do violence, pray;
Today is short, tomorrow nigh:

Why will you die? why will you die?
You sinned with me a pleasant sin:
Repent with me, for I repent.
Woe's me the lore I must unlearn!
Woe's me that easy way we went,
So rugged when I would return!
How long until my sleep begin,
How long shall stretch these nights and days?
Surely, clean Angels cry, she prays;
She laves her soul with tedious tears:
How long must stretch these years and years?

I turn from you my cheeks and eyes,
My hair which you shall see no more—
Alas for joy that went before,
For joy that dies, for love that dies.
Only my lips still turn to you,
My livid lips that cry, Repent.
Oh weary life, Oh weary Lent,
Oh weary time whose stars are few.

How should I rest in Paradise,
Or sit on steps of heaven alone?
If Saints and Angels spoke of love
Should I not answer from my throne:
Have pity upon me, ye my friends,
For I have heard the sound thereof:

Should I not turn with yearning eyes,
Turn earthwards with a pitiful pang?
Oh save me from a pang in heaven.
By all the gifts we took and gave,
Repent, repent, and be forgiven:
This life is long, but yet it ends;
Repent and purge your soul and save:
No gladder song the morning stars
Upon their birthday morning sang
Then Angels sing when one repents.

I tell you what I dreamed last night:
A spirit with transfigured face
Fire-footed clomb an infinite space.
I heard his hundred pinions clang,
Heaven-bells rejoicing rang and rang,
Heaven-air was thrilled with subtle scents,
Worlds spun upon their rushing cars:
He mounted shrieking: "Give me light."
Still light was poured on him, more light;
Angels, Archangels he outstripped
Exultant in exceeding might,
And trod the skirts of Cherubim.
Still "Give me light," he shrieked; and dipped
His thirsty face, and drank a sea,
Athirst with thirst it could not slake.
I saw him, drunk with knowledge, take

From aching brows the aureole crown —
His locks writhed like a cloven snake —
He left his throne to grovel down
And lick the dust of Seraphs' feet:
For what is knowledge duly weighed?
Knowledge is strong, but love is sweet;
Yea all the progress he had made
Was but to learn that all is small
Save love, for love is all in all.

I tell you what I dreamed last night:
It was not dark, it was not light,
Cold dews had drenched my plenteous hair
Thro' clay; you came to seek me there.
And "Do you dream of me?" you said.
My heart was dust that used to leap
To you; I answered half asleep:
"My pillow is damp, my sheets are red,
There's a leaden tester to my bed:
Find you a warmer playfellow,
A warmer pillow for your head,
A kinder love to love than mine."
You wrung your hands; while I like lead
Crushed downwards thro' the sodden earth:
You smote your hands but not in mirth,
And reeled but were not drunk with wine.
For all night long I dreamed of you:

I woke and prayed against my will,
Then slept to dream of you again.
At length I rose and knelt and prayed:
I cannot write the words I said,
My words were slow, my tears were few;
But thro' the dark my silence spoke
Like thunder. When this morning broke,
My face was pinched, my hair was grey,
And frozen blood was on the sill
Where stifling in my struggle I lay.

If now you saw me you would say:
Where is the face I used to love?
And I would answer: Gone before;
It tarries veiled in paradise.
When once the morning star shall rise,
When earth with shadows flees away
And we stand safe within the door,
Then you shall lift the veil thereof.
Look up, rise up: for far above
Our palms are grown, our place is set;
There we shall meet as once we met
And love with old familiar love.

WINTER RAIN

Every valley drinks,
  Every dell and hollow:
Where the kind rain sinks and sinks,
  Green of Spring will follow.

Yet a lapse of weeks
  Buds will burst their edges,
Strip their wool-coats, glue-coats, streaks,
  In the woods and hedges;

Weave a bower of love
  For birds to meet each other,
Weave a canopy above
  Nest and egg and mother.

But for fattening rain
  We should have no flowers,
Never a bud or leaf again
  But for soaking showers;

Never a mated bird
  In the rocking tree-tops,
Never indeed a flock or herd
  To graze upon the lea-crops.

Lambs so woolly white,
  Sheep the sun-bright leas on,
They could have no grass to bite
  But for rain in season.

We should find no moss
  In the shadiest places,
Find no waving meadow grass
  Pied with broad-eyed daisies:

But miles of barren sand,
  With never a son or daughter,
Not a lily on the land,
  Or lily on the water.

SPRING

Frost-locked all the winter,
Seeds, and roots, and stones of fruits,
What shall make their sap ascend
That they may put forth shoots?
Tips of tender green,
Leaf, or blade, or sheath;
Telling of the hidden life
That breaks forth underneath,
Life nursed in its grave by Death.

Blows the thaw-wind pleasantly,
Drips the soaking rain,
By fits looks down the waking sun:
Young grass springs on the plain;
Young leaves clothe early hedgerow trees;
Seeds, and roots, and stones of fruits,
Swollen with sap put forth their shoots;
Curled-headed ferns sprout in the lane;
Birds sing and pair again.

There is no time like Spring,
When life's alive in everything,
Before new nestlings sing,
Before cleft swallows speed their journey back
Along the trackless track —

God guides their wing,
He spreads their table that they nothing lack,—
Before the daisy grows a common flower,
Before the sun has power
To scorch the world up in his noontide hour.

There is no time like Spring,
Like Spring that passes by;
There is no life like Spring-life born to die,—
Piercing the sod,
Clothing the uncouth clod,
Hatched in the nest,
Fledged on the windy bough,
Strong on the wing:
There is no time like Spring that passes by,
Now newly born, and now
Hastening to die.

GOBLIN MARKET

Morning and evening
Maids heard the goblins cry:
"Come buy our orchard fruits,
Come buy, come buy:
Apples and quinces,
Lemons and oranges,
Plump unpecked cherries,
Melons and raspberries,
Bloom-down-cheeked peaches,
Swart-headed mulberries,
Wild free-born cranberries,
Crab-apples, dewberries,
Pine-apples, blackberries,
Apricots, strawberries; —
All ripe together
In summer weather, —
Morns that pass by,
Fair eves that fly;
Come buy, come buy:
Our grapes fresh from the vine,
Pomegranates full and fine,
Dates and sharp bullaces,
Rare pears and greengages,
Damsons and bilberries,
Taste them and try:

Currants and gooseberries,
Bright-fire-like barberries,
Figs to fill your mouth,
Citrons from the South,
Sweet to tongue and sound to eye;
Come buy, come buy."

Evening by evening
Among the brookside rushes,
Laura bowed her head to hear,
Lizzie veiled her blushes:
Crouching close together
In the cooling weather,
With clasping arms and cautioning lips,
With tingling cheeks and finger tips.
"Lie close," Laura said,
Pricking up her golden head:
"We must not look at goblin men,
We must not buy their fruits:
Who knows upon what soil they fed
Their hungry thirsty roots?"
"Come buy," call the goblins
Hobbling down the glen.
"Oh," cried Lizzie, "Laura, Laura,
You should not peep at goblin men."
Lizzie covered up her eyes,
Covered close lest they should look;

Laura reared her glossy head,
And whispered like the restless brook:
"Look, Lizzie, look, Lizzie,
Down the glen tramp little men.
One hauls a basket,
One bears a plate,
One lugs a golden dish
Of many pounds weight.
How fair the vine must grow
Whose grapes are so luscious;
How warm the wind must blow
Thro' those fruit bushes."
"No," said Lizzie: "No, no, no;
Their offers should not charm us,
Their evil gifts would harm us."
She thrust a dimpled finger
In each ear, shut eyes and ran:
Curious Laura chose to linger
Wondering at each merchant man.
One had a cat's face,
One whisked a tail,
One tramped at a rat's pace,
One crawled like a snail,
One like a wombat prowled obtuse and furry,
One like a ratel tumbled hurry skurry.
She heard a voice like voice of doves
Cooing all together:

They sounded kind and full of loves
In the pleasant weather.
Laura stretched her gleaming neck
Like a rush-imbedded swan,
Like a lily from the beck,
Like a moonlit poplar branch,
Like a vessel at the launch
When its last restraint is gone.

Backwards up the mossy glen
Turned and trooped the goblin men,
With their shrill repeated cry,
"Come buy, come buy."
When they reached where Laura was
They stood stock still upon the moss,
Leering at each other,
Brother with queer brother;
Signalling each other,
Brother with sly brother.
One set his basket down,
One reared his plate;
One began to weave a crown
Of tendrils, leaves and rough nuts brown
(Men sell not such in any town);
One heaved the golden weight
Of dish and fruit to offer her:
"Come buy, come buy," was still their cry.

Laura stared but did not stir,
Longed but had no money:
The whisk-tailed merchant bade her taste
In tones as smooth as honey,
The cat-faced purr'd,
The rat-paced spoke a word
Of welcome, and the snail-paced even was heard;
One parrot-voiced and jolly
Cried "Pretty Goblin" still for "Pretty Polly;"—
One whistled like a bird.

But sweet-tooth Laura spoke in haste:
"Good folk, I have no coin;
To take were to purloin:
I have no copper in my purse,
I have no silver either,
All my gold is on the furze
That shakes in windy weather
Above the rusty heather."
"You have much gold upon your head,"
They answered all together:
"Buy from us with a golden curl."
She clipped a precious golden lock,
She dropped a tear more rare than pearl,
Then sucked their fruit globes fair or red:
Sweeter than honey from the rock.
Stronger than man-rejoicing wine,

Clearer than water flowed that juice;
She never tasted such before,
How should it cloy with length of use?
She sucked and sucked and sucked the more
Fruits which that unknown orchard bore;
She sucked until her lips were sore;
Then flung the emptied rinds away
But gathered up one kernel-stone,
And knew not was it night or day
As she turned home alone.

Lizzie met her at the gate
Full of wise upbraidings:
"Dear, you should not stay so late,
Twilight is not good for maidens;
Should not loiter in the glen
In the haunts of goblin men.
Do you not remember Jeanie,
How she met them in the moonlight,
Took their gifts both choice and many,
Ate their fruits and wore their flowers
Plucked from bowers
Where summer ripens at all hours?
But ever in the noonlight
She pined and pined away;
Sought them by night and day,
Found them no more but dwindled and grew grey;

Then fell with the first snow,
While to this day no grass will grow
Where she lies low:
I planted daisies there a year ago
That never blow.
You should not loiter so."
"Nay, hush," said Laura:
"Nay, hush, my sister:
I ate and ate my fill,
Yet my mouth waters still;
Tomorrow night I will
Buy more:" and kissed her:
"Have done with sorrow;
I'll bring you plums tomorrow
Fresh on their mother twigs,
Cherries worth getting;
You cannot think what figs
My teeth have met in,
What melons icy-cold
Piled on a dish of gold
Too huge for me to hold,
What peaches with a velvet nap,
Pellucid grapes without one seed:
Odorous indeed must be the mead
Whereon they grow, and pure the wave they drink
With lilies at the brink,
And sugar-sweet their sap."

Golden head by golden head,
Like two pigeons in one nest
Folded in each other's wings,
They lay down in their curtained bed:
Like two blossoms on one stem,
Like two flakes of new-fall'n snow,
Like two wands of ivory
Tipped with gold for awful kings.
Moon and stars gazed in at them,
Wind sang to them lullaby,
Lumbering owls forbore to fly,
Not a bat flapped to and fro
Round their rest:
Cheek to cheek and breast to breast
Locked together in one nest.

Early in the morning
When the first cock crowed his warning,
Neat like bees, as sweet and busy,
Laura rose with Lizzie:
Fetched in honey, milked the cows,
Aired and set to rights the house,
Kneaded cakes of whitest wheat,
Cakes for dainty mouths to eat,
Next churned butter, whipped up cream,
Fed their poultry, sat and sewed;
Talked as modest maidens should:

Lizzie with an open heart,
Laura in an absent dream,
One content, one sick in part;
One warbling for the mere bright day's delight,
One longing for the night.

At length slow evening came:
They went with pitchers to the reedy brook;
Lizzie most placid in her look,
Laura most like a leaping flame.
They drew the gurgling water from its deep;
Lizzie plucked purple and rich golden flags,
Then turning homewards said: "The sunset flushes
Those furthest loftiest crags;
Come, Laura, not another maiden lags,
No wilful squirrel wags,
The beasts and birds are fast asleep."
But Laura loitered still among the rushes
And said the bank was steep.

And said the hour was early still,
The dew not fall'n, the wind not chill:
Listening ever, but not catching
The customary cry,
"Come buy, come buy,"
With its iterated jingle
Of sugar-baited words:

Not for all her watching
Once discerning even one goblin
Racing, whisking, tumbling, hobbling;
Let alone the herds
That used to tramp along the glen,
In groups or single,
Of brisk fruit-merchant men.
Till Lizzie urged, "O Laura, come;
I hear the fruit-call but I dare not look:
You should not loiter longer at this brook:
Come with me home.
The stars rise, the moon bends her arc,
Each glowworm winks her spark,
Let us get home before the night grows dark:
For clouds may gather
Tho' this is summer weather,
Put out the lights and drench us thro';
Then if we lost our way what should we do?"

Laura turned cold as stone
To find her sister heard that cry alone,
That goblin cry,
"Come buy our fruits, come buy."
Must she then buy no more such dainty fruit?
Must she no more such succous pasture find,
Gone deaf and blind?
Her tree of life drooped from the root:

She said not one word in her heart's sore ache;
But peering thro' the dimness, nought discerning,
Trudged home, her pitcher dripping all the way;
So crept to bed, and lay
Silent till Lizzie slept;
Then sat up in a passionate yearning,
And gnashed her teeth for baulked desire, and wept
As if her heart would break.

Day after day, night after night,
Laura kept watch in vain
In sullen silence of exceeding pain.
She never caught again the goblin cry:
"Come buy, come buy;"—
She never spied the goblin men
Hawking their fruits along the glen:
But when the noon waxed bright
Her hair grew thin and gray;
She dwindled, as the fair full moon doth turn
To swift decay and burn
Her fire away.

One day remembering her kernel-stone
She set it by a wall that faced the south;
Dewed it with tears, hoped for a root,
Watched for a waxing shoot,
But there came none;

It never saw the sun,
It never felt the trickling moisture run:
While with sunk eyes and faded mouth
She dreamed of melons, as a traveller sees
False waves in desert drouth
With shade of leaf-crowned trees,
And burns the thirstier in the sandful breeze.
She no more swept the house,
Tended the fowls or cows,
Fetched honey, kneaded cakes of wheat,
Brought water from the brook:
But sat down listless in the chimney–nook
And would not eat.

Tender Lizzie could not bear
To watch her sister's cankerous care
Yet not to share.
She night and morning
Caught the goblins' cry:
"Come buy our orchard fruits,
Come buy, come buy:" —
Beside the brook, along the glen,
She heard the tramp of goblin men,
The voice and stir
Poor Laura could not hear;
Longed to buy fruit to comfort her,
But feared to pay too dear.

She thought of Jeanie in her grave,
Who should have been a bride;
But who for joys brides hope to have
Fell sick and died
In her gay prime,
In earliest Winter time,
With the first glazing rime,
With the first snow-fall of crisp Winter time.
Till Laura dwindling
Seemed knocking at Death's door:
Then Lizzie weighed no more
Better and worse;
But put a silver penny in her purse,
Kissed Laura, crossed the heath with clumps of
  furze
At twilight, halted by the brook:
And for the first time in her life
Began to listen and look.

Laughed every goblin
When they spied her peeping:
Came towards her hobbling,
Flying, running, leaping,
Puffing and blowing,
Chuckling, clapping, crowing,
Clucking and gobbling,
Mopping and mowing,

Full of airs and graces,
Pulling wry faces,
Demure grimaces,
Cat-like and rat-like,
Ratel- and wombat-like,
Snail-paced in a hurry,
Parrot-voiced and whistler,
Helter skelter, hurry skurry,
Chattering like magpies,
Fluttering like pigeons,
Gliding like fishes, —
Hugged her and kissed her,
Squeezed and caressed her:
Stretched up their dishes,
Panniers, and plates:
"Look at our apples
Russet and dun,
Bob at our cherries,
Bite at our peaches,
Citrons and dates,
Grapes for the asking,
Pears red with basking
Out in the sun,
Plums on their twigs;
Pluck them and suck them,
Pomegranates, figs." —

"Good folk," said Lizzie,
Mindful of Jeanie:
"Give me much and many:"—
Held out her apron,
Tossed them her penny.
"Nay, take a seat with us,
Honour and eat with us,"
They answered grinning:
"Our feast is but beginning.
Night yet is early,
Warm and dew-pearly,
Wakeful and starry:
Such fruits as these
No man can carry;
Half their bloom would fly,
Half their dew would dry,
Half their flavour would pass by.
Sit down and feast with us,
Be welcome guest with us,
Cheer you and rest with us."—
"Thank you," said Lizzie: "But one waits
At home alone for me:
So without further parleying,
If you will not sell me any
Of your fruits tho' much and many,
Give me back my silver penny
I tossed you for a fee."—

They began to scratch their pates,
No longer wagging, purring,
But visibly demurring,
Grunting and snarling.
One called her proud,
Cross-grained, uncivil;
Their tones waxed loud,
Their looks were evil.
Lashing their tails
They trod and hustled her,
Elbowed and jostled her,
Clawed with their nails,
Barking, mewing, hissing, mocking,
Tore her gown and soiled her stocking,
Twitched her hair out by the roots,
Stamped upon her tender feet,
Held her hands and squeezed their fruits
Against her mouth to make her eat.
White and golden Lizzie stood,
Like a lily in a flood, —
Like a rock of blue-veined stone
Lashed by tides obstreperously, —
Like a beacon left alone
In a hoary roaring sea.
Sending up a golden fire, —
Like a fruit-crowned orange-tree
White with blossoms honey-sweet

Sore beset by wasp and bee, —
Like a royal virgin town
Topped with gilded dome and spire
Close beleagured by a fleet
Mad to tug her standard down.

One may lead a horse to water,
Twenty cannot make him drink.
Tho' the goblins cuffed and caught her,
Coaxed and fought her,
Bullied and besought her,
Scratched her, pinched her black as ink,
Kicked and knocked her,
Mauled and mocked her,
Lizzie uttered not a word;
Would not open lip from lip
Lest they should cram a mouthful in:
But laughed in heart to feel the drip
Of juice that syrupped all her face,
And lodged in dimples of her chin,
And streaked her neck which quaked like curd.
At last the evil people
Worn out by her resistance
Flung back her penny, kicked their fruit
Along whichever road they took,
Not leaving root or stone or shoot;
Some writhed into the ground,

Some dived into the brook
With ring and ripple,
Some scudded on the gale without a sound,
Some vanished in the distance.

In a smart, ache, tingle,
Lizzie went her way;
Knew not was it night or day;
Sprang up the bank, tore thro' the furze,
Threaded copse and dingle,
And heard her penny jingle
Bouncing in her purse,
Its bounce was music to her ear.
She ran and ran
As if she feared some goblin man
Dogged her with gibe or curse
Or something worse:
But not one goblin skurried after,
Nor was she pricked by fear;
The kind heart made her windy-paced
That urged her home quite out of breath with haste
And inward laughter.

She cried "Laura," up the garden,
"Did you miss me?
Come and kiss me.
Never mind my bruises,

Hug me, kiss me, suck my juices
Squeezed from goblin fruits for you,
Goblin pulp and goblin dew.
Eat me, drink me, love me;
Laura, make much of me:
For your sake I have braved the glen
And had to do with goblin merchant men."

Laura started from her chair,
Flung her arms up in the air,
Clutched her hair:
"Lizzie, Lizzie, have you tasted
For my sake the fruit forbidden?
Must your light like mine be hidden,
Your young life like mine be wasted,
Undone in mine undoing
And ruined in my ruin,
Thirsty, cankered, goblin-ridden?"—
She clung about her sister,
Kissed and kissed and kissed her:
Tears once again
Refreshed her shrunken eyes,
Dropping like rain
After long sultry drouth;
Shaking with aguish fear, and pain,
She kissed and kissed her with a hungry mouth.

Her lips began to scorch,
That juice was wormwood to her tongue,
She loathed the feast:
Writhing as one possessed she leaped and sung,
Rent all her robe, and wrung
Her hands in lamentable haste,
And beat her breast.
Her locks streamed like the torch
Borne by a racer at full speed,
Or like the mane of horses in their flight,
Or like an eagle when she stems the light
Straight toward the sun,
Or like a caged thing freed,
Or like a flying flag when armies run.

Swift fire spread thro' her veins, knocked at her
heart,
Met the fire smouldering there
And overbore its lesser flame;
She gorged on bitterness without a name:
Ah! fool, to choose such part
Of soul-consuming care!
Sense failed in the mortal strife:
Like the watch-tower of a town
Which an earthquake shatters down,
Like a lightning-stricken mast,
Like a wind-uprooted tree

Spun about,
Like a foam-topped waterspout
Cast down headlong in the sea,
She fell at last;
Pleasure past and anguish past,
Is it death or is it life?

Life out of death.
That night long Lizzie watched by her,
Counted her pulse's flagging stir,
Felt for her breath,
Held water to her lips, and cooled her face
With tears and fanning leaves:
But when the first birds chirped about their eaves,
And early reapers plodded to the place
Of golden sheaves,
And dew-wet grass
Bowed in the morning winds so brisk to pass,
And new buds with new day
Opened of cup-like lilies on the stream,
Laura awoke as from a dream,
Laughed in the innocent old way,
Hugged Lizzie but not twice or thrice;
Her gleaming locks showed not one thread of grey,
Her breath was sweet as May
And light danced in her eyes.
Days, weeks, months, years

Afterwards, when both were wives
With children of their own;
Their mother-hearts beset with fears,
Their lives bound up in tender lives;
Laura would call the little ones
And tell them of her early prime,
Those pleasant days long gone
Of not-returning time:
Would talk about the haunted glen,
The wicked, quaint fruit-merchant men,
Their fruits like honey to the throat
But poison in the blood;
(Men sell not such in any town:)
Would tell them how her sister stood
In deadly peril to do her good,
And win the fiery antidote:
Then joining hands to little hands
Would bid them cling together,
"For there is no friend like a sister
In calm or stormy weather;
To cheer one on the tedious way,
To fetch one if one goes astray,
To lift one if one totters down,
To strengthen whilst one stands."

PASSING AWAY

Passing away, saith the World, passing away:
Chances, beauty and youth sapped day by day:
Thy life never continueth in one stay.
Is the eye waxen dim, is the dark hair changing to
  grey
That hath won neither laurel nor bay?
I shall clothe myself in Spring and bud in May:
Thou, root-stricken, shalt not rebuild thy decay
On my bosom for aye.
Then I answered: Yea.

Passing away, saith my Soul, passing away:
With its burden of fear and hope, of labour and
  play;
Hearken what the past doth witness and say:
Rust in thy gold, a moth is in thine array,
A canker is in thy bud, thy leaf must decay.
At midnight, at cockcrow, at morning, one certain
  day
Lo the bridegroom shall come and shall not delay:
Watch thou and pray.
Then I answered: Yea.

Passing away, saith my God, passing away:
Winter passeth after the long delay:

New grapes on the vine, new figs on the tender
spray,
Turtle calleth turtle in Heaven's May.
Tho' I tarry, wait for Me, trust Me, watch and
pray.
Arise, come away, night is past and lo it is day,
My love, My sister, My spouse, thou shalt hear
Me say.
Then I answered: Yea.

MIRAGE

The hope I dreamed of was a dream,
  Was but a dream; and now I wake
Exceeding comfortless, and worn, and old,
    For a dream's sake.

I hang my harp upon a tree,
  A weeping willow in a lake;
I hang my silenced harp there, wrung and snapt
    For a dream's sake.

Lie still, lie still, my breaking heart;
  My silent heart, lie still and break:
Life, and the world, and mine own self, are
      changed
    For a dream's sake.

"NO, THANK YOU, JOHN"

I never said I loved you, John:
  Why will you teaze me day by day,
And wax a weariness to think upon
    With always "do" and "pray"?

You know I never loved you, John;
  No fault of mine made me your toast:
Why will you haunt me with a face as wan
    As shows an hour-old ghost?

I dare say Meg or Moll would take
  Pity upon you, if you'd ask:
And pray don't remain single for my sake
    Who can't perform that task.

I have no heart?—Perhaps I have not;
  But then you're mad to take offence
That I don't give you what I have not got:
    Use your own common sense.

Let bygones be bygones:
  Don't call me false, who owed not to be true:
I'd rather answer "No" to fifty Johns
    Than answer "Yes" to you.

Let's mar our pleasant days no more,
  Song-birds of passage, days of youth:
Catch at today, forget the days before:
    I'll wink at your untruth.

Let us strike hands as hearty friends;
  No more, no less; and friendship's good:
Only don't keep in view ulterior ends,
    And points not understood

In open treaty. Rise above
  Quibbles and shuffling off and on:
Here's friendship for you if you like; but love, —
    No, thank you, John.

PROMISES LIKE PIE-CRUST

Promise me no promises,
  So will I not promise you:
Keep we both our liberties,
  Never false and never true:
Let us hold the die uncast,
  Free to come as free to go:
For I cannot know your past,
  And of mine what can you know?

You, so warm, may once have been
  Warmer towards another one:
I, so cold, may once have seen
  Sunlight, once have felt the sun:
Who shall show us if it was
  Thus indeed in time of old?
Fades the image from the glass,
  And the fortune is not told.

If you promised, you might grieve
  For lost liberty again:
If I promised, I believe
  I should fret to break the chain:
Let us be the friends we were,
  Nothing more but nothing less:
Many thrive on frugal fare
  Who would perish of excess.

THE LOWEST PLACE

Give me the lowest place: not that I dare
  Ask for that lowest place, but Thou hast died
That I might live and share
  Thy glory by Thy side.

Give me the lowest place: or if for me
  That lowest place too high, make one more low
Where I may sit and see
  My God and love Thee so.

SOMEWHERE OR OTHER

Somewhere or other there must surely be
  The face not seen, the voice not heard,
The heart that not yet — never yet — ah me!
    Made answer to my word.

Somewhere or other may be near or far:
  Past land and sea, clean out of sight:
Beyond the wandering moon, beyond the star
    That tracks her night by night.

Somewhere or other, may be far or near;
  With just a wall, a hedge, between;
With just the last leaves of the dying year
    Fallen on a turf grown green.

DESPISED AND REJECTED

My sun has set, I dwell
In darkness as a dead man out of sight;
And none remains, not one, that I should tell
To him mine evil plight
This bitter night.
I will make fast my door
That hollow friends may trouble me no more.

"Friend, open to Me."—Who is this that calls?
Nay, I am deaf as are my walls:
Cease crying, for I will not hear
Thy cry of hope or fear.
Others were dear,
Others forsook me: what art thou indeed
That I should heed
Thy lamentable need?
Hungry should feed,
Or stranger lodge thee here?

"Friend, My Feet bleed.
Open thy door to Me and comfort Me."
I will not open, trouble me no more.
Go on thy way footsore,
I will not rise and open unto thee.

"Then is it nothing to thee? Open, see
Who stands to plead with thee.
Open, lest I should pass thee by, and thou
One day entreat My Face
And howl for grace,
And I be deaf as thou art now.
Open to Me."

Then I cried out upon him: Cease,
Leave me in peace:
Fear not that I should crave
Aught thou mayst have.
Leave me in peace, yea trouble me no more,
Lest I arise and chase thee from my door.
What, shall I not be let
Alone, that thou dost vex me yet?

But all night long that voice spake urgently:
"Open to Me."
Still harping in mine ears:
"Rise, let Me in."
Pleading with tears:
"Open to Me that I may come to thee."
While the dew dropped, while the dark hours were
  cold
"My Feet bleed, see My Face,
See My Hands bleed that bring thee grace,

My Heart doth bleed for thee,
Open to Me."
So till the break of day:
Then died away
That voice, in silence as of sorrow;
Then footsteps echoing like a sigh
Passed me by,
Lingering footsteps slow to pass.
On the morrow
I saw upon the grass
Each footprint marked in blood, and on my door
The mark of blood for evermore.

GROWN AND FLOWN

I loved my love from green of Spring
  Until sere Autumn's fall;
But now that leaves are withering
  How should one love at all?
  One heart's too small
For hunger, cold, love, everything.

I loved my love on sunny days
  Until late Summer's wane;
But now that frost begins to glaze
  How should one love again?
  Nay, love and pain
Walk wide apart in diverse ways.

I loved my love — alas to see
  That this should be, alas!
I thought that this could scarcely be,
  Yet has it come to pass:
  Sweet sweet love was,
Now bitter bitter grown to me.

TWICE

I took my heart in my hand
  (O my love, O my love),
I said: Let me fall or stand,
  Let me live or die,
But this once hear me speak—
  (O my love, O my love)—
Yet a woman's words are weak;
  You should speak, not I.

You took my heart in your hand
  With a friendly smile,
With a critical eye you scanned,
  Then set it down,
And said: It is still unripe,
  Better wait awhile;
Wait while the skylarks pipe,
  Till the corn grows brown.

As you set it down it broke—
  Broke, but I did not wince;
I smiled at the speech you spoke,
  At your judgment that I heard:
But I have not often smiled
  Since then, nor questioned since,
Nor cared for corn-flowers wild,
  Nor sung with the singing bird.

I take my heart in my hand,
  O my God, O my God,
My broken heart in my hand:
  Thou hast seen, judge Thou.
My hope was written on sand,
  O my God, O my God;
Now let Thy judgment stand—
  Yea, judge me now.

This contemned of a man,
  This marred one heedless day,
This heart take Thou to scan
  Both within and without:
Refine with fire its gold,
  Purge Thou its dross away—
Yea hold it in Thy hold,
  Whence none can pluck it out.

I take my heart in my hand—
  I shall not die, but live—
Before Thy face I stand;
  I, for Thou callest such:
All that I have I bring,
  All that I am I give,
Smile Thou and I shall sing,
  But shall not question much.

DOST THOU NOT CARE?

I love and love not: Lord, it breaks my heart
  To love and not to love.
Thou veiled within Thy glory, gone apart
  Into Thy shrine, which is above,
Dost Thou not love me, Lord, or care
  For this mine ill? —
I love thee here or there,
  I will accept thy broken heart, lie still.

Lord, it was well with me in time gone by
  That cometh not again,
When I was fresh and cheerful, who but I?
  I fresh, I cheerful: worn with pain
Now, out of sight and out of heart;
  O Lord, how long? —
I watch thee as thou art,
  I will accept thy fainting heart, be strong.

"Lie still," "be strong," today; but, Lord,
   tomorrow,
   What of tomorrow, Lord?
Shall there be rest from toil, be truce from sorrow,
   Be living green upon the sward
Now but a barren grave to me,
   Be joy for sorrow? —
Did I not die for thee?
   Do I not live for thee? leave Me *tomorrow.*

WEARY IN WELL-DOING

I would have gone; God bade me stay:
  I would have worked; God bade me rest.
He broke my will from day to day,
  He read my yearnings unexpressed
    And said them nay.

Now I would stay; God bids me go:
  Now I would rest; Gods bid me work.
He breaks my heart tossed to and fro,
  My soul is wrung with doubts that lurk
    And vex it so.

I go, Lord, where Thou sendest me;
  Day after day I plod and moil:
But, Christ my God, when will it be
  That I may let alone my toil
    And rest with Thee?

A DIRGE

Why were you born when the snow was falling?
You should have come to the cuckoo's calling,
Or when grapes are green in the cluster,
Or, at least, when lithe swallows muster
        For their far off flying
        From summer dying.

Why did you die when the lambs were cropping?
You should have died at the apples' dropping,
When the grasshopper comes to trouble,
And the wheat-fields are sodden stubble,
        And all winds go sighing
        For sweet things dying.

IF ONLY

If I might only love my God and die!
  But now He bids me love Him and live on,
  Now when the bloom of all my life is gone,
The pleasant half of life has quite gone by.
My tree of hope is lopped that spread so high;
  And I forget how Summer glowed and shone,
  While Autumn grips me with its fingers wan,
And frets me with its fitful windy sigh.
When Autumn passes then must Winter numb,
  And Winter may not pass a weary while,
    But when it passes Spring shall flower again:
  And in that Spring who weepeth now shall smile,
    Yea, they shall wax who now are on the wane,
Yea, they shall sing for love when Christ shall come.

SHALL I FORGET?

Shall I forget on this side of the grave?
I promise nothing: you must wait and see
Patient and brave.
(O my soul, watch with him and he with me.)

Shall I forget in peace of Paradise?
I promise nothing: follow, friend, and see
Faithful and wise.
(O my soul, lead the way he walks with me.)

FROM SUNSET TO STAR RISE

Go from me, summer friends, and tarry not:
I am no summer friend, but wintry cold,
A silly sheep benighted from the fold,
A sluggard with a thorn-choked garden plot.
Take counsel, sever from my lot your lot,
Dwell in your pleasant places, hoard your gold;
Lest you with me should shiver on the wold,
Athirst and hungering on a barren spot.

For I have hedged me with a thorny hedge,
I live alone, I look to die alone:
Yet sometimes when a wind sighs through the sedge
Ghosts of my buried years and friends come back,
My heart goes sighing after swallows flown
On sometime summer's unreturning track.

AMOR MUNDI

"Oh where are you going with your love-locks
    flowing
  On the west wind blowing along this valley
    track?"
"The downhill path is easy, come with me an it
    please ye,
  We shall escape the uphill by never turning
    back."

So they two went together in glowing August
    weather,
  The honey-breathing heather lay to their left and
    right;
And dear she was to doat on, her swift feet seemed
    to float on
  The air like soft twin pigeons too sportive to
    alight.

"Oh what is that in heaven where grey cloud-
    flakes are seven,
  Where blackest clouds hang riven just at the
    rainy skirt?"
"Oh that's a meteor sent us, a message dumb,
    portentous,
  An undeciphered solemn signal of help or hurt."

"Oh what is that glides quickly where velvet flowers grow thickly,
Their scent comes rich and sickly?" — "A scaled and hooded worm."
"Oh what's that in the hollow, so pale I quake to follow?"
"Oh that's a thin dead body which waits the eternal term."

"Turn again, O my sweetest, — turn again, false and fleetest:
This beaten way thou beatest I fear is hell's own track."
"Nay, too steep for hill-mounting; nay, too late for cost-counting:
This downhill path is easy, but there's no turning back."

AUTUMN VIOLETS

Keep love for youth, and violets for the spring:
  Or if these bloom when worn-out autumn
      grieves,
  Let them lie hid in double shade of leaves,
Their own, and others dropped down withering;
For violets suit when home birds build and sing,
  Not when the outbound bird a passage cleaves;
  Not with dry stubble of mown harvest sheaves,
But when the green world buds to blossoming.
Keep violets for the spring, and love for youth,
  Love that should dwell with beauty, mirth, and
      hope:
    Or if a later sadder love be born,
    Let this not look for grace beyond its scope,
  But give itself, nor plead for answering truth —
      A grateful Ruth tho' gleaning scanty corn.

"THEY DESIRE A BETTER COUNTRY"

I

I would not if I could undo my past,
  Tho' for its sake my future is a blank;
  My past for which I have myself to thank,
For all its faults and follies first and last.
I would not cast anew the lot once cast,
  Or launch a second ship for one that sank,
  Or drug with sweets the bitterness I drank,
Or break by feasting my perpetual fast.
I would not if I could: for much more dear
  Is one remembrance than a hundred joys,
    More than a thousand hopes in jubilee;
    Dearer the music of one tearful voice
      That unforgotten calls and calls to me,
    "Follow me here, rise up, and follow here."

II

What seekest thou, far in the unknown land?
  In hope I follow joy gone on before;
  In hope and fear persistent more and more,
As the dry desert lengthens out its sand.
Whilst day and night I carry in my hand
  The golden key to ope the golden door
  Of golden home; yet mine eye weepeth sore,
For long the journey is that makes no stand.
And who is this that veiled doth walk with thee?
  Lo, this is Love that walketh at my right;
    One exile holds us both, and we are bound
  To selfsame home-joys in the land of light.
    Weeping thou walkest with him; weepeth
      he? —
    Some sobbing weep, some weep and make no
      sound.

III

A dimness of a glory glimmers here
  Thro' veils and distance from the space remote,
  A faintest far vibration of a note
Reaches to us and seems to bring us near;
Causing our face to glow with braver cheer,
  Making the serried mist to stand afloat,
  Subduing languor with an antidote,
And strengthening love almost to cast out fear:
Till for one moment golden city walls
  Rise looming on us, golden walls of home,
Light of our eyes until the darkness falls;
  Then thro' the outer darkness burdensome
I hear again the tender voice that calls,
  "Follow me hither, follow, rise, and come."

CONFLUENTS

As rivers seek the sea,
  Much more deep than they,
So my soul seeks thee
  Far away:
As running rivers moan
On their course alone,
  So I moan
  Left alone.

As the delicate rose
  To the sun's sweet strength
Doth herself unclose,
  Breadth and length;
So spreads my heart to thee
Unveiled utterly,
  I to thee
  Utterly.

As morning dew exhales
  Sunwards pure and free,
So my spirit fails
  After thee:
As dew leaves not a trace
On the green earth's face;
  I, no trace
  On thy face.

Its goal the river knows,
  Dewdrops find a way,
Sunlight cheers the rose
  In her day:
Shall I, lone sorrow past,
Find thee at last?
  Sorrow past,
  Thee at last?

MONNA INNOMINATA
A Sonnet of Sonnets

Beatrice, immortalized by "altissimo poeta . . . cotanto amante"; Laura, celebrated by a great tho' an inferior bard,—have alike paid the exceptional penalty of exceptional honour, and have come down to us resplendent with charms, but (at least, to my apprehension) scant of attractiveness.

These heroines of world-wide fame were preceded by a bevy of unnamed ladies "donne innominate" sung by a school of less conspicuous poets; and in that land and that period which gave simultaneous birth to Catholics, to Albigenses, and to Troubadours, one can imagine many a lady as sharing her lover's poetic aptitude, while the barrier between them might be one held sacred by both, yet not such as to render mutual love incompatible with mutual honour.

Had such a lady spoken for herself, the portrait left us might have appeared more tender, if less dignified, than any drawn even by a devoted friend. Or had the Great Poetess of our own day and nation only been unhappy instead of happy, her circumstances would have invited her to bequeath to us, in lieu of the "Portuguese Sonnets", an inimitable "donna innominata" drawn not from fancy but from feeling, and worthy to occupy a niche beside Beatrice and Laura.

MONNA INNOMINATA

1.

"Lo dì che han detto a' dolci amici addio." — DANTE.
"Amor, con quanto sforzo oggi mi vinci!" — PETRARCA.

Come back to me, who wait and watch for you: —
  Or come not yet, for it is over then,
  And long it is before you come again,
So far between my pleasures are and few.
While, when you come not, what I do I do
  Thinking "Now when he comes," my sweetest
    "when:"
  For one man is my world of all the men
This wide world holds; O love, my world is you.
Howbeit, to meet you grows almost a pang
  Because the pang of parting comes so soon;
My hope hangs waning, waxing, like a moon
  Between the heavenly days on which we meet:
Ah me, but where are now the songs I sang
  When life was sweet because you called them
    sweet?

2.

"Era già l'ora che volge il desio." —DANTE.
"Ricorro al tempo ch'io vi vidi prima." —PETRARCA.

I wish I could remember that first day,
First hour, first moment of your meeting me,
If bright or dim the season, it might be
Summer or Winter for aught I can say;
So unrecorded did it slip away,
So blind was I to see and to foresee,
So dull to mark the budding of my tree
That would not blossom yet for many a May.
If only I could recollect it, such
A day of days! I let it come and go
As traceless as a thaw of bygone snow;
It seemed to mean so little, meant so much;
If only now I could recall that touch,
First touch of hand in hand—Did one but
know!

3.

"O ombre vane, fuor che ne l'aspetto!"—DANTE.
"Immaginata guida la conduce."—PETRARCA.

I dream of you to wake: would that I might
  Dream of you and not wake but slumber on;
  Nor find with dreams the dear companion gone,
As Summer ended Summer birds take flight.
In happy dreams I hold you full in sight,
  I blush again who waking look so wan;
  Brighter than sunniest day that ever shone,
In happy dreams your smile makes day of night.
Thus only in a dream we are at one,
  Thus only in a dream we give and take
    The faith that maketh rich who take or give;
  If thus to sleep is sweeter than to wake,
    To die were surely sweeter than to live,
Tho' there be nothing new beneath the sun.

4.

"Poca favilla gran fiamma seconda." — DANTE.
"Ogni altra cosa, ogni pensier va fore,
E sol ivi con voi rimansi amore." — PETRARCA.

I loved you first: but afterwards your love
Outsoaring mine, sang such a loftier song
As drowned the friendly cooings of my dove.
Which owes the other most? my love was long,
And yours one moment seemed to wax more
strong;
I loved and guessed at you, you construed me
And loved me for what might or might not be —
Nay, weights and measures do us both a wrong.
For verily love knows not "mine" or "thine;"
With separate "I" and "thou" free love has done,
For one is both and both are one in love:
Rich love knows nought of "thine that is not
mine;"
Both have the strength and both the length
thereof,
Both of us, of the love which makes us one.

5.

"Amor che a nulla amato amar perdona." — DANTE.
"Amor m'addusse in sì gioiosa spene." — PETRARCA.

O my heart's heart, and you who are to me
  More than myself myself, God be with you,
  Keep you in strong obedience leal and true
To Him whose noble service setteth free,
Give you all good we see or can foresee,
  Make your joys many and your sorrows few,
  Bless you in what you bear and what you do,
Yea, perfect you as He would have you be.
So much for you; but what for me, dear friend?
  To love you without stint and all I can
Today, tomorrow, world without an end;
    To love you much and yet to love you more,
  As Jordan at his flood sweeps either shore;
Since woman is the helpmeet made for man.

6.

"Or puoi la quantitate
Comprender de l'amor che a te mi scalda."—DANTE.
"Non vo'che da tal nodo amor mi scioglia."—PETRARCA.

Trust me, I have not earned your dear rebuke,
I love, as you would have me, God the most;
Would lose not Him, but you, must one be lost,
Nor with Lot's wife cast back a faithless look
Unready to forego what I forsook;
This say I, having counted up the cost,
This, tho' I be the feeblest of God's host,
The sorriest sheep Christ shepherds with His crook.
Yet while I love my God the most, I deem
That I can never love you overmuch;
I love Him more, so let me love you too;
Yea, as I apprehend it, love is such
I cannot love you if I love not Him,
I cannot love Him if I love not you.

7.

"Qui primavera sempre ed ogni frutto."—DANTE.
"Ragionando con meco ed io con lui."—PETRARCA.

"Love me, for I love you"—and answer me,
"Love me, for I love you"—so shall we stand
As happy equals in the flowering land
Of love, that knows not a dividing sea.
Love builds the house on rock and not on sand,
Love laughs what while the winds rave desperately;
And who hath found love's citadel unmanned?
And who hath held in bonds love's liberty?
My heart's a coward tho' my words are brave—
We meet so seldom, yet we surely part
So often; there's a problem for your art!
Still I find comfort in his Book, who saith,
Tho' jealousy be cruel as the grave,
And death be strong, yet love is strong as death.

8.

"Come dicesse a Dio: D'altro non calme." — DANTE.
"Spero trovar pietà non che perdono." — PETRARCA.

"I, if I perish, perish" — Esther spake:
And bride of life or death she made her fair
In all the lustre of her perfumed hair
And smiles that kindle longing but to slake.
She put on pomp of loveliness, to take
Her husband thro' his eyes at unaware;
She spread abroad her beauty for a snare,
Harmless as doves and subtle as a snake.
She trapped him with one mesh of silken hair,
She vanquished him by wisdom of her wit,
And built her people's house that it should stand: —
If I might take my life so in my hand,
And for my love to Love put up my prayer,
And for love's sake by Love be granted it!

9.

"O dignitosa coscienza e netta!" — DANTE.
"Spirto più acceso di virtuti ardenti." — PETRARCA.

Thinking of you, and all that was, and all
That might have been and now can never be,
I feel your honoured excellence, and see
Myself unworthy of the happier call:
For woe is me who walk so apt to fall,
So apt to shrink afraid, so apt to flee,
Apt to lie down and die (ah, woe is me!)
Faithless and hopeless turning to the wall.
And yet not hopeless quite nor faithless quite,
Because not loveless; love may toil all night,
But take at morning; wrestle till the break
Of day, but then wield power with God and man: —
So take I heart of grace as best I can,
Ready to spend and be spent for your sake.

10.

"Con miglior corso e con migliore stella." — DANTE.
"La vita fugge e non s'arresta un' ora." — PETRARCA.

Time flies, hope flags, life plies a wearied wing;
  Death following hard on life gains ground apace;
  Faith runs with each and rears an eager face,
Outruns the rest, makes light of everything,
Spurns earth, and still finds breath to pray and sing;
  While love ahead of all uplifts his praise,
  Still asks for grace and still gives thanks for grace.
Content with all day brings and night will bring.
Life wanes; and when love folds his wings above
  Tired hope, and less we feel his conscious pulse,
    Let us go fall asleep, dear friend, in peace:
    A little while, and age and sorrow cease;
  A little while, and life reborn annuls
Loss and decay and death, and all is love.

11.

"Vien dietro a me e lascia dir le genti." — DANTE.
"Contando i casi della vita nostra." — PETRARCA.

Many in aftertimes will say of you
"He loved her" — while of me what will they say?
Not that I loved you more than just in play,
For fashion's sake as idle women do.
Even let them prate; who know not what we knew
Of love and parting in exceeding pain.
Of parting hopeless here to meet again,
Hopeless on earth, and heaven is out of view.
But by my heart of love laid bare to you.
My love that you can make not void nor vain,
Love that foregoes you but to claim anew
Beyond this passage of the gate of death,
I charge you at the Judgment make it plain
My love of you was life and not a breath.

12.

"Amor, che ne la mente mi ragiona." — DANTE.
"Amor vien nel bel viso di costei." — PETRARCA.

If there be any one can take my place
  And make you happy whom I grieve to grieve,
  Think not that I can grudge it, but believe
I do commend you to that nobler grace,
That readier wit than mine, that sweeter face;
  Yea, since your riches make me rich, conceive
  I too am crowned, while bridal crowns I weave,
And thread the bridal dance with jocund pace.
For if I did not love you, it might be
  That I should grudge you some one dear delight;
    But since the heart is yours that was mine own,
    Your pleasure is my pleasure, right my right,
  Your honourable freedom makes me free,
      And you companioned I am not alone.

13.

"E drizzeremo gli' occhi al Primo Amore," — DANTE.
"Ma trovo peso non da le mie braccia." — PETRARCA.

If I could trust mine own self with your fate,
  Shall I not rather trust it in God's hand?
  Without Whose Will one lily doth not stand,
Nor sparrow fall at his appointed date;
  Who numbereth the innumerable sand,
Who weighs the wind and water with a weight,
To Whom the world is neither small nor great,
  Whose knowledge foreknew every plan we
    planned,
Searching my heart for all that touches you,
  I find there only love and love's goodwill
Helpless to help and impotent to do,
    Of understanding dull, of sight most dim;
    And therefore I commend you back to Him
  Whose love your love's capacity can fill.

14.

"E la Sua Volontade è nostra pace." — DANTE.
"Sol con questi pensier, con altre chiome." — PETRARCA.

Youth gone, and beauty gone if ever there
  Dwelt beauty in so poor a face as this;
  Youth gone and beauty, what remains of bliss?
I will not bind fresh roses in my hair,
To shame a cheek at best but little fair, —
  Leave youth his roses, who can bear a thorn, —
I will not seek for blossoms anywhere,
  Except such common flowers as blow with corn.
Youth gone and beauty gone, what doth remain?
  The longing of a heart pent up forlorn,
    A silent heart whose silence loves and longs;
    The silence of a heart which sang its songs
  While youth and beauty make a summer morn,
Silence of love that cannot sing again.

LATER LIFE - SONNET 17

Something this foggy day, a something which
Is neither of this fog nor of today,
Has set me dreaming of the winds that play
Past certain cliffs, along one certain beach,
And turn the topmost edge of waves to spray:
Ah pleasant pebbly strand so far away,
So out of reach while quite within my reach,
As out of reach as India or Cathay!
I am sick of where I am and where I am not,
I am sick of foresight and of memory,
I am sick of all I have and all I see,
I am sick of self, and there is nothing new;
Oh weary impatient patience of my lot!—
Thus with myself: how fares it, Friends, with you?

"SUMMER IS ENDED"

To think that this meaningless thing was ever a
rose,
Scentless, colourless, *this*!
Will it ever be thus (who knows?)
Thus with our bliss,
If we wait till the close?

Tho' we care not to wait for the end, there comes
the end
Sooner, later, at last,
Which nothing can mar, nothing mend:
An end locked fast,
Bent we cannot re-bend.

SLEEPING AT LAST

Sleeping at last, the trouble and tumult over,
  Sleeping at last, the struggle and horror past,
Cold and white, out of sight of friend and of lover,
            Sleeping at last.

  No more a tired heart downcast or overcast,
No more pangs that wring or shifting fears that
    hover,
  Sleeping at last in a dreamless sleep locked fast.

Fast asleep. Singing birds in their leafy cover
  Cannot wake her, nor shake her the gusty blast.
Under the purple thyme and the purple clover
            Sleeping at last.